COULD A PENGUIN RIDE A BIKE?

...and other questions

Aleksei Bitskoff &
Camilla de la
Bédoyère

QEB Publishing

A penguin is a bird that can swim, but cannot fly.

Design: Duck Egg Blue
Editor: Ruth Symons
Editorial Director: Victoria Garrard
Art Director: Laura Roberts-Jensen

Copyright © QEB Publishing 2015

First published in the United States by
QEB Publishing, Inc.
3 Wrigley, Suite A
Irvine, CA 92618

A CIP record for this book is available from the
Library of Congress.

ISBN 978 1 60992 734 9

Printed in China

King penguins live on islands near the South Pole.

It is freezing cold, and bitter winds blow hard across the snow.

Imagine if a king penguin came to stay. What would he do?

Could a penguin play soccer?

He might think the ball is
an egg.
He would hide it under his
fluffy tummy feathers to
keep it warm!

A king penguin carries his egg on his feet to keep it off the ground.

Moms and dads take turns looking after the egg for two months, until it hatches.

A baby penguin is called a

chick.

What if a penguin went to the swimming pool?

Penguins love to swim, so he would dive right in.

He would use his wings like flippers to fly through the water.

Penguins are **excellent swimmers.**

They can swim **four times faster** than the fastest human swimmers.

Penguins can stay underwater for **five minutes** at a time.

What if a baby penguin came for dinner?

He might try to **eat everything!**

An adult penguin eats about **50 fish** a day, but a chick needs to eat about **200!**

That's because chicks grow a thick layer of fat
to keep them warm in the icy weather.

What if a penguin went bowling?

He wouldn't be able to throw a ball. He doesn't have fingers or hands. He has wings instead.

Who needs a ball anyway?

Penguins love to slide on their tummies along the ice—it's called tobogganing.

Whoosh

It's so much quicker than waddling!

Could a penguin ride a bike?

A penguin would fall off a bike. His legs are **too short** to reach the pedals!

But he would be **zoom-tastic** on a scooter.

He could also do cool tricks on a skateboard!

Penguins have wide, webbed feet.

They are great at **balancing** because they live on slippery rocks and ice.

What if a penguin went on a picnic?

He wouldn't need to pack a picnic basket.

At lunchtime, he would throw up stinky fish from his tummy and share them with everyone.

Yum!

Penguin parents swallow fish at sea—and then throw them up to feed their chicks.

Could a penguin join a chorus?

He would sound TERRIBLE!

Some birds sing beautifully, but not penguins.

♪ WONK!
WONK!
♪ WONK!
WONK!

Penguins and chicks honk, squawk, and whistle so they can find each other in a crowd.

What if a penguin went to the supermarket?

He would feel right at home in the cold aisle.

A penguin's island home is even colder than the **inside of a fridge!**

Penguins' bodies are covered in feathers, which work like a **thick blanket** to keep them warm.

When chicks get cold, they huddle together in big groups called crèches.

What if a penguin stayed overnight?

He wouldn't want to stay in the guest bedroom. Penguins get too lonely by themselves.

In some places, ONE MILLION penguins
live together in a big group called a colony.

A penguin wouldn't need a bed or a sleeping bag.
Penguins sleep standing up, with their beaks
tucked under their wings.

More about penguins

King Penguin is pointing to the places where he lives. Can you see where you live?

FACT FILE

There are 17 different types of penguin. The largest ones are emperor penguins. King penguins are the second largest.

Penguins have black and white waterproof feathers.

Most penguins live in cold places, but some types live in places where the weather is warm, such as South Africa.

Penguins eat fish, shellfish, and squid. They swim fast to catch their food.

While other birds have wings for flying, penguins have flippers to help them swim in the water.

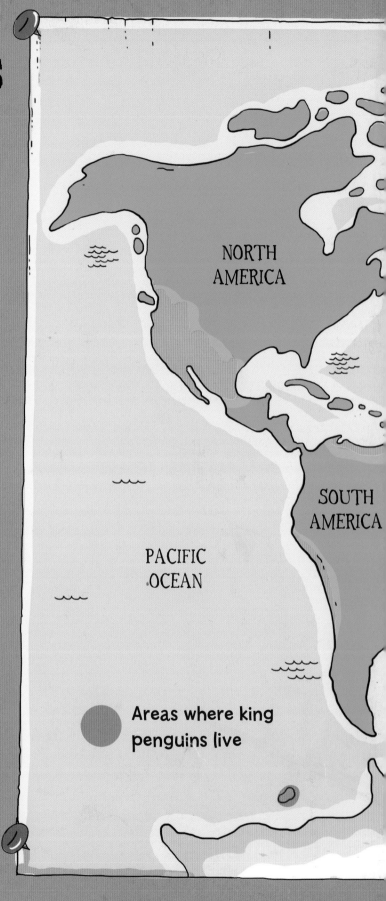

NORTH AMERICA

SOUTH AMERICA

PACIFIC OCEAN

Areas where king penguins live

Greetings from Antarctica!

POST CARD

I am back home now, on my snow-covered island near the South Pole. It's lovely and cold, and I can spend all day diving into the sea. I had yummy fish for breakfast, lunch, and dinner yesterday—and it's great to be back with my family!

See you soon.

Love, King Penguin ✕

SENT BY KING PENGUIN POST
ST. ANDREW'S BAY, SOUTH GEORGIA

The Jones Family
72 Main Street
Anytown
12345
USA

1704092201112

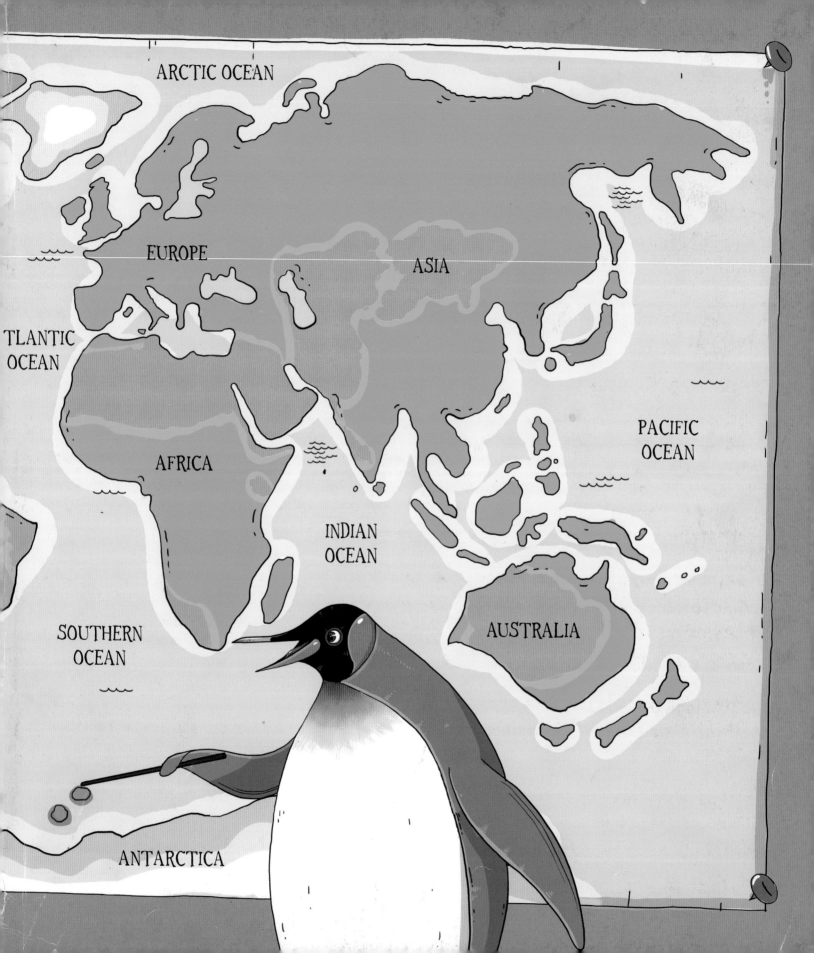